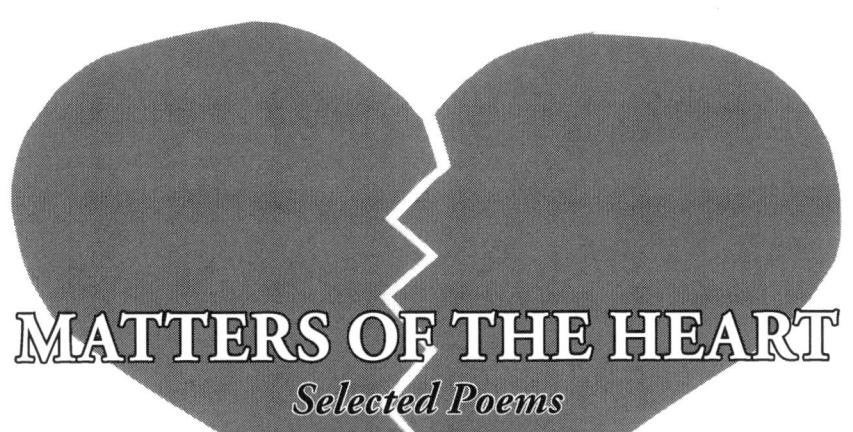

MATTERS OF THE HEART
Selected Poems

Poems By
S. Glenn Wakefield

authorHOUSE®

AuthorHouse™
1663 Liberty Drive
Bloomington, IN 47403
www.authorhouse.com
Phone: 1 (800) 839-8640

© *2006 S. Glenn Wakefield. All rights reserved.*

No part of this book may be reproduced, stored in a retrieval system, or transmitted by any means without the written permission of the author.

Published by AuthorHouse 09/09/2015

ISBN: 978-1-4259-0569-9 (sc)
ISBN: 978-1-4670-6812-3 (e)

Print information available on the last page.

Any people depicted in stock imagery provided by Thinkstock are models, and such images are being used for illustrative purposes only. Certain stock imagery © Thinkstock.

This book is printed on acid-free paper.

Because of the dynamic nature of the Internet, any web addresses or links contained in this book may have changed since publication and may no longer be valid. The views expressed in this work are solely those of the author and do not necessarily reflect the views of the publisher, and the publisher hereby disclaims any responsibility for them.

These poems are dedicated to

Susan Whittlesey who saw me through an epiphany

Where I realized I could not find inner peace by avoiding conflict.

Special thanks to Ethelene and Roland West who made it all possible.

Table of Contents

WHAT IS LOVE? 1

LOOKING AT THE ROSES 27

ACTING ON THE STAGE OF LIFE 47

A CALL TO ARMS 81

THE AMERICAN WAY 101

WHAT IS LOVE?

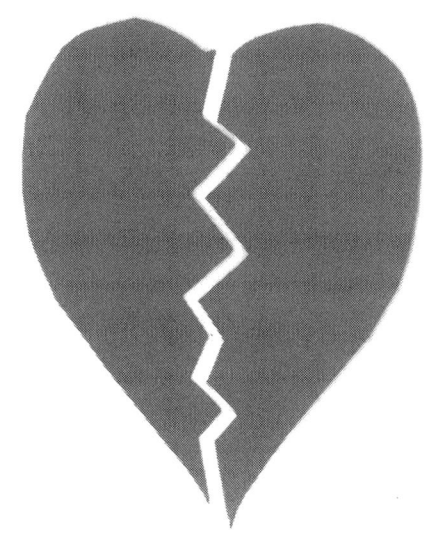

WHAT IS LOVE

My day starts and ends with thoughts of you
If I couldn't see you, what would I do?
My heart flutters when you walk by
I stutter, lost for words and I don't know why
When you look at another I want to cry
Without you there is no moon, no sunshine
There is blackness; it is night all the time
If you left me the birds won't sing and the flowers won't bloom
It would be darkness, total gloom
What love is, I don't know, I don't care?
To tell you how I feel, I'm afraid, I wouldn't dare
If I spend a day without seeing you
I would be lost; I wouldn't know what to do

I LOVE YOU

Matters of the heart differ from those of the mind
Any fool knows they are not of a kind
When you love some one you must tell them so
If you are loved in return it is good to know
If I could choose, I would be a dove
Because I know they share true love
You cannot choose your family, only friends
So carefully choose the one you love, you should always win
If they don't love you
It does not stop the fire in your heart that burns
Let her go, if you really love her
If she comes back; pray it's her final choice and not just a whim
There is always hope for all mankind
Because a broken heart will heal with time

LOVE IS JUST A MIRAGE

It's my feelings, my thoughts they are not real
Part of a dream
Fart of a cruel scheme
      Love is just a mirage
Why must my feelings betray my heart?
Why must my feelings betray my thoughts?
Why must my feelings betray my soul?
      Love is just a mirage
My thoughts are about you, every minute each day
My thoughts are your safety
My thoughts are about losing you
      Love is just a mirage
You can't be real, I wish I could get you out of my mind
You can't be real, I wish I could be with you unto eternity
You can"t be real, I wish this dream would go away
      Love is just a mirage

A CRAZY LOVE

I am thinking of her as I start the day
She's in my thought. Visions of her won't go away
I wish her happiness, life's many joys
I want for her all of life's little toys
I want to give her all the things money can and can't buy
How do you tell someone; how do I tell her how deeply I care?
How do you admit it to yourself; how much of your soul do you bare?
Love makes you lose your sense of direction and forget all your goals
It will make you leave your family and your best friends and walk on hot coals
It makes you forget to eat your meals
At work you can't think, love clouds your mind and your business deals
When you live to make her happy and that's all your life means
When her image is in your mind every second and at night in your dreams
You're hopelessly and truly in love.
Thank God it's the end of this work day
I better go home, lie down and hope that these crazy love feelings will go away

WHY CAN'T I MAKE YOU LOVE ME

Why couldn't I make you love me?
Why couldn't I make you stay?
Why did you leave me? Why did you go away?
I wish I could put all this in the past
But the hollow feeling in my stomach lasts and lasts
You're looking for someone who is different and deep
You want someone to listen to you talk and hold you while you sleep
My heart is shattered because I know you'll find someone new
I only hope they love you half as much as I do
The tears roll down my cheeks and fall into space
They splatter on the wax floor like a crystal vase
I can't forget you it will take years and years
There may be a time you'll kiss away these tears
But you can't make someone love you and it breaks my heart to say
The more I smothered you with love, the more I pushed you away

LOVE OF MY LIFE
I MISS YOU

I miss you like the blossoms of Spring
You were my path through the forest, my everything
I miss you like the autumn leaves
You're my fresh air, like a summer breeze
I miss you like rain on a April shower
You're my umbrella, my little sunflower
I miss you like white Christmas I know
You're my shelter from the falling snow
I miss you my log fire in freezing cold
In my body, in my heart and in my soul
I miss you beside me every night
In the darkness, you were my light
I miss you every second we're apart
Only you can mend my broken heart

DARK BROWN EYES

The first time I saw you I was lost to this world
I would give up everything for you to be my girl
I realize now that it was too high a price
A love that left me hope to find in death what I missed in life
When I looked into those deep set dark brown eyes
I wondered what they were hiding, what secrets, what lies
You looked at me, I could not say no, when you cried
I believed everything you said, even when you lied
I gave up my family and all of my friends for you. It was too high a cost
One realizes the depth of love only when it's lost
Those dark circles, that fixed look, that stare
I wondered what they knew, I was afraid to ask
Whirlpools of danger, the windows of your soul
Those dark brown eyes with stories untold
You disappeared, you left without a trace
I looked for you everywhere, I cried in public, my disgrace
Life is not fair; sometimes you must let some things pass
When you have love you live for every second and make the moment last

MY COUNTRY GIRL

I believe my Girl don't appreciate me, she's just after my money
That girl don't know what's happening, I got a surprise for that honey
I ain't got no money, ain't got no house, ain't got no car
I got a hound dog, a Ford pick-up and a stogie cigar
I love my stogies, my dog, my truck, my beer in that order
And I ain't changing nothing come hell or high water
Ain't had a steady job in over a year
But I do odd jobs to buy my beer
Ah she want is my money, that woman can be a bitter pill
They gonna take back the rented furniture if she don't pay that bill
All she does is complain about the bills and bad luck
I helps by doing them odd jobs now and then to earn a buck
I wish she'd change that complaint record and sing a different song
Or I'm on the road again cause I've been around here to long
She makes the payments on the trailer and she's been such a dear
And I'm gonna give her one more chance; I'll make that clear
If not, I'm taking my stogies, my dog and putting my truck in gear
Cause I got a full tank of gas and I'm out of here

A BAD DREAM

In my dream I can't eat, can't sleep, I wake up and I'm a long way from home
Now is my time to heal, to think while things are quiet and I'm all alone
The deep pain I feel from misplaced love and the betrayal of the original sin
I'm dealing with because we all die some time; it's only a matter of when
My lover's plan to leave me was somewhat less than clever
My mind will not let me forget it, not now, not today, not ever
She was young, suffered grief and I know how far she's come
I must forgive her gall, but I can not forget what she has done
My dear, your lover can pray to his God or talk to him personally, that's up to you
So it's best you keep him out of my face because you know what I'll do
I loved you like no other; you had my full and lasting devotion
Please stay away, I need some time and space to deal with my emotions
I am lost for words and I don't know what more to say
I will never forget. In time I will forgive you, but not today!

DO YOU LOVE ME

Do you love me How much do you care
How much will you give How much will you share
Are we the ideal couple; are we a matched pair
Will you hold my hand when we walk in the park
Will you let me kiss you in the moonlight when it's dark
Will you be my one and only and always my best friend
Can I depend on you forever through thick and thin
Because I want some one with me to the very end
Will you stand by me no matter what the cost
Or will you forsake me when all I have is lost
Do you love me How much do you care
How much will you give How much do you dare
Will you tell me your secrets about your love affairs
Will you have my baby and go back to work to pay the bills
Or will you hang around the house, get fat and go back on the pill
Will you get out of bed when you don't feel well
And cook the meals and rub my back or tell me to go to hell
Will you comfort me when I'm in despair and there seems to be no hope
Or will you call your friends and tell them you married a worthless dope
Will you go to work when I've lost my job
Or will you complain to your father and others that I'm just a slob
Do you love me How much do you care
How much will you give How much will you share
I want you to love me above all others or is that not fair
I need some one who believes in me to stand by my side
Through the ups and downs and cling to me with pride
Will you be proud to be with me when my hair is gray
Will we laugh and take out old pictures of our wedding day
If your answer is yes, let's go through life together
I don't want someone who is with me only in fair weather

Truth, love, respect and support is what I promise you for the rest of our days
I only ask the same from you, for now, the future, beyond and for always
Do you love me How much do you care
How much will you give How much do you dare
I will love you above all others; we are a matched pair

DESPAIR

How much should I suffer? How long should I wait?
What did I not do? What could I have done? What could I have said?
I told you how I feel. You know who I am
Must I stay in the shadows? Can I step into the light?
When is the hope gone? When does reality set in?
Hearts are broken, time does not stop, we must move on
To cross an ocean or a dessert, to climb a mountain
Is it enough? Your heart belongs to another
                              Your thoughts are not of me
Why can't I walk away? Why can't I see?
Turn around, one more glance, it will have to hold me an eternity
There is always hope but some things are not to be
Cast your bread upon the water. There are other fish in the sea
But I know in my heart there is only one girl for me

LOST BAGGAGE

You came to me with open arms
You had beauty and many charms
What you brought to the relationship was distress
You had plenty of baggage, your life was a mess
Now, I know people are a total package, their baggage can't be lost
Let it be, because a commitment to them comes at too high a cost
If you only knew then what you know now, you would have wished
she had passed you by
The heartache she caused was enough to make a grown man cry
Some people can't loose their baggage, They just can't be saved
And the pain they inflict can haunt you to your grave
Living life is drawing a line with ink without an eraser
If you make a mistake, talk to your love, you face her
If the relationship is wrong, move on and find someone new
The world is large, there are many sights to see, places to go and things to do
You can't take her baggage and throw it away
She carries it from her past into her future and deals with it everyday

WHEN LOVE IS ENOUGH

When you have broken my heart and trample on all my dreams
When everything I've ever wanted comes apart at the seams
When you have slept with all the men of your choosing
When your angel image is just an illusion
I know love is not enough
Not enough to hold us together
Not enough to make us one
Not enough to bind us forever
I have a love for you like I have never known
The candle of love lit in my heart for you will always burn
When people talk about you, I don't want my children to come home and cry
When I walk down the street, I don't want to see that knowing look in a man's eye
I know love is not enough
Not enough to hold us together
Not enough to make us one
Not enough to bind us forever
The mother of my children is special in every way
Children should be proud of their mother every day
We know in the good and bad times she will always be there
On all occasions we depend on her because she is the one who will care
I know love is enough
Enough to hold us together
Enough to make us one
Enough to bind us forever

THE AFFAIR

You left me, I was lonely, I was blue
I thought the best day of my life was the day I met you
I was lost in a cloud of purple haze, I didn't know what to do
Now, I know the best day of my life was the last day I saw you
You came into my life like a hurricane
Everything in my world was turned upside down
I knew without you I didn't want to live
Like a little puppy, I followed you around
You left me, I was lonely, I was blue
I thought the best day of my life was the day I met you
I was lost in a cloud of purple haze, I didn't know what to do
Now, I know the best day of my life was the last day I saw you
I look at your empty pillow and cry
My love is an abyss, I want you to be with me as I grow old
Walking to work only strangers can see me cry
This love is eternal, it is deep, I feel it in my soul
You left me, I was lonely, I was blue
I thought the best day of my life was the day I met you
I was lost in a cloud of purple haze, I didn't know what to do
Now, I know the best day of my life was the last day I saw you

ON THE BEACH

A
Time in the sun
A time you should have fun
The seagulls fly low it is food they seek
Put your suntan lotion on or you may burn
But it's my head that throbs and my stomach that churns
I'm moving on, putting you out of my mind. I'm going to forget you
It is time to think of all the good things, when I had a great time
I must look back, think of how we met, you were a real find
I wish you well in all of your future endeavors
You have a great mind you are very clever
Choose wisely, you are willing and able
Your life should be a story book fable
I hope the best is yet to come
You will make a choice
I know it will be
The right
One

WHAT IS LOVE / REALITY

I have eyes and I can see but I only see what I want to see
I have ears and I can hear but I only hear what I want to hear
They say you are not beautiful but you are beautiful to me
They say you are unfaithful but to me you are as true as you can be
Is love blind and deaf; do we see and hear what we want to believe?
When we are young we see, we hear, we speak
When we are adults we see things but we don't speak
When we are adults we hear things but we do not speak
Do we see life clearer as a child or as an adult?
When we become adults we put away childish things
Are the glasses of adults filtered for survival?
Are we told what to believe?
Or do we believe what we are told?

THANK YOU FOR YOUR TIME

We were driving down the road of life; pull over please, stop the car
Let me out at the curb; with you I know, I've traveled too far
I wanted a partner for life and you acted like a juvenile
I was looking for a wife and I found an immature child
I look back at our relationship to see what I lost
A grain of sand from the beach of eternity was the cost
I look forward to gray hair, false teeth and faded hope
I fell in love with a troubled person who couldn't cope
My heart is in pieces and my headaches bring pain
I don't know why you played me or for what gain
You hung me like a wet reticule, on a clothesline to dry
I wonder? I wonder? Yes, I still wonder; why?
You ignored my feelings, like a pile of dirty dishes
You didn't honor my love and made fun of my wishes
I kissed you, held you. You called me your man
You really didn't care and you still don't know who I am

THE BIG GIRL

Why can't I change the things I see?
From the way they are to the way I want them to be
Why can't I, why can't I, why can't I
Why can't I change your heart?
You know I love you but it doesn't matter to you
You hurt yourself, you hurt me too
Why do you do the things you do?
I don't know why life is so cruel
Why don't people follow the golden rule?
But you are out there in the die hard world
You are an adult, you're not a little girl
The serenity prayer says I have no power over many things
I miss you, the longing, the throbbing in my head makes my ears ring
I would like to protect you from all of the pain
The bad times, the weather, the snow and the rain
Why can't I, why can't I, why can't I
But the path of life lies out there
You must learn from your mistakes that life is unfair

WHAT IS TRUE LOVE?

Know that I will love you forever, know that I always will
That is a frightening commitment and it can be a bitter pill
Knowing in your heart I love you and I've done all I can
What if you should fall in love with another man?
If you told me this, would I tell you to go to hell?
Or through the pain could I think about it and wish you well?
Maybe the love would help me to wish you both the best
If I really love you isn't that the final test?

A LOST SOUL

My first love, your misdeeds and the pain that you have cost
The betrayal, the hurt, you'll never fully know about the love that you lost
Some stumble through life without guilt or shame
They care only for themselves, taking from others not remembering their names
They drive down the hill of broken hearts and don't look in the rear view mirror
At the shattered lives left behind
Do they sense the despair, will these people realize the harm they cause,
Will they know this in do time
Some people hurt others to take away or pass on their pain
They should know it doesn't stop their suffering and these efforts are in vain
I was hurt deeply and the ache won't go away
I woke up crying and I trying to make it through the day
I going to move on, I'll find happiness and live life to the letter
Out there is a new love, I'll find her and things will get better
I'll always remember you, my first love; if you wish to ask me for forgiveness now, don't
God will forgive in heaven but in this world, I won't

A TOUCH OF CLASS

Why does love makes one helpless, it's debilitating and it's blind
Why can't the brain absorb, digest and process the truth in time
When your dreams are shattered life becomes cruel, life is unfair
Why can't we sense mendacity and smell the deceit in the air
I saw you only as I wanted you to be
Not the way you were
Now I see you the way you are
Not the way I wanted you to be
I must look back and see what I saw in you
Not much depth, just me, me, me, not much understanding of reality
Can life be lived with no sense of value of worth or meaning?
                        Yes, it can
Can life be lived without honesty, respect and pride?
                        Yes, it can
How would living with a person devoid of these traits be?
Day by day, day in, day out, a minute can be eternity
I don't want anyone who doesn't respect, honor and have pride in me
A person must have self-respect, self-worth, to bring to my table
If not, I don't want you in my heart, my home
                        Not now, not ever

WHO AM I?

I am not your father, I am not your mother
I am not your sister, I am not your brother
Who am I
I am one who loves freely and with fear of pain
I know deep in my soul there really is no shame
Who am I
If I love someone, I will tell them so
If someone loved me, I would want to know
Who am I
My love was rejected, so I cry in the dark
I am in despair with my broken heart
Who am I
I am falling through space, my life frozen in time
Some day you may love someone enough, to give them this rhyme

I WILL ALWAYS BE WAITING

I can only hope and pray
That on the brightest day
Or on the darkest night
I hope you will come back
I hold my breath and pray
On the warmest day
Or on the coldest night
I hope you will come back
As long as the sun rises
As long as the moon glows
As long as I breathe
I will wait for you
The door is always open
I know some day you will come back

LOOKING AT THE ROSES

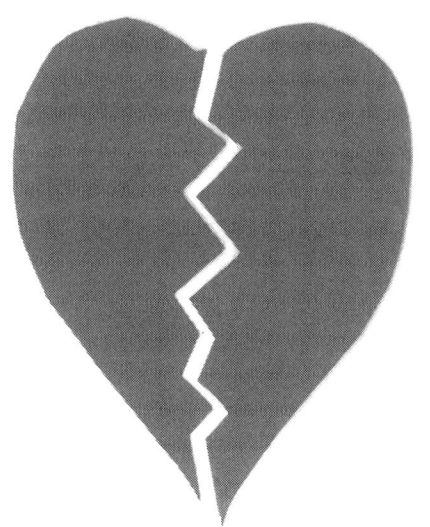

A VACATION

I've left the city for the country because it's so beautiful and green
I don't miss the subway, the bright lights and the streets that are mean
Somehow, I feel guilty, I'm not in the office working at a frantic pace
But I am curious to see how things will develop in this new place
I look out the window and see the distant lake but the sky is very gray
There is an overhang of clouds, the sun is hiding on this dreary day
Where are the birds that sing
This is April is it not? It is early spring
Are the birds unhappy with the weather, where are they today
Maybe they are all asleep, I hope they have not flown away
This is a well deserved vacation, I'll shave and put on some lotion
It's good to be away from those street lights, loud sirens, the city commotion
On second thought, it's too quiet and I don't feel totally comfortable here
Maybe I need more noise but I know there's nothing to fear
I'll try to relax and enjoy the silence and this down time
While I'm away from the rat race, the city closeness and the petty crime
What a view, some tops have been cut out of the huge evergreen trees
The sun comes through the bay window, outside it's brighter than it seems
And under the window is a large garden of many colored posies
I'll stop, look around and take time to smell the roses

SUMMER

Summer it is the best time of the year; I'll state my case
Think of the warm light coming through the bay window on your face,
School vacations, going to the beach and walks in the park
Holding hands, sitting on the porch swing, while stealing a kiss in the dark
Looking up I seeing birds returning from their winter stay
Traveling north, flying through the night; they have come a long way
The bees are hopping from flower to flower
They are collecting pollen hour after hour
A long day of work, and they return to their hive all tuckered out
But you can be sure they will be back tomorrow, there is not doubt
I enjoy a picnic basket with my girl under the trees
I enjoy watching the squirrels playing and busy working bees
The female birds are looking at the males, they want to pick the best
Some have made a choice and are ready to build their nest
This is truly the best season of the year.
I don't need my coat, my scarf or my winter gear
The squirrels and the birds and bees
Are having fun as they frolic in the trees
They all have aglow, which comes from above
We are all very happy because we're in love

NOT TO BE

I really loved you once this is not hard to see
But Honey some things are just not to be
Every time I was happy and things were alright
You would make hateful comments and start a fight
When I married you, you were pretty and thin
You were the carnival Barbie-Doll on the self I wanted to win
Your hips were narrow and your breast were large
Now from the rear you look like a river barge
Now you are wrinkled, fat and gray
You look like the Raggedy Anne Doll I threw away
You yelled at me and hit me in front of the kids
I wanted to call you a "B" and one time I did
You threw pots and pans at me and said don't come back
You packed all my things in a croaker sack
I'm just a country boy trying to do his best
But baby I can't pass this test
For better or worse is what I said
I ain't staying in this, I'd rather be dead
You know you are worse than I married you far
I'm taking the pick up but I'm leaving you the car
I'm heading West like the writer Thomas Mann
Where there's plenty of space and lots of land
I really loved you once this is not hard to see
But Honey some things are just not to be

OLD AGE
HAPY BIRTHDAY

As we get older, we must know
Our steps grow shorter, as we go
Our hair gets gray or maybe white
As our eyes get weaker, as we loose clear sight
Some people get fat while others get thinner
We can all go to heaven if we're not a sinner
Our children grow up and they leave the nest
We can only pray that we've done our best
Life's journey for some is short, for other it's long
Whoever keeps the time clock can't be wrong
For someone with a heart of gold
With family and friends made along the way
I hope you are happy on this special day
HAPPY BIRTHDAY

BABY JOHN

I'm up very early, looking forward to this day
My daughter and my grandson are on their way
I watch him grow a little every day
I love this time with him, I must say
On her way to work his mother is dropping him off today
I can pick him up or put him in the walker or his pen to play
The rooms have been made child proof, so I can get a breath of rest
Baby John pulls down everything, putting my patience to a test
Everything goes in his mouth, he's getting teeth and growing hair
He's into everything and I watch him every second, It's called being aware
I watch him grow a little every day
I love this time with him, I must say
I feed him, I change him, I love him, I care
He's curious, he's playful, he's my little teddy bear
When he takes his nap, I can get my chores done
When I finish and he wakes up, we can have some more fun
I'm tired because it has been a long day
Soon my daughter will come and take baby John away
I watch him grow a little everyday
I love this time with him, I must say

MY FRIEND MARY

I have known you for a very long time
And I'm proud to say you're a friend of mine
You find few people who are so good it's a sin
Maybe it's a relative or maybe it's just a friend
What ever the qualities that this person shares
It makes them special and someone who cares
Life for most of us is very short at best
We all want to go to heaven, if we past the final test
In this time frame, ups and downs will appear
But I can always depend on you year after year
It has been a pleasure knowing someone like you, that's for sure
You're kind and warm to everyone because your heart's so pure
I look up at your head and I see lots of white snow
You meet many people in life but you're the most beautiful person I know

A NEW BABY

What did I have? Tell me Doctor what is this child
Tell me what it is so I can smile
Tell me, if it is a boy or a girl
If it's a boy it will make my world
If it's a girl as beautiful as it's mother
We will try again to give her a brother
Sir, the baby is healthy and the mother is fine
Doctor, I want a namesake, a one of a kind
If it's a girl it's OK, but a boy would be better
A boy would play rough, a girl would knit me a sweater
A girl would love her father when he got old
She would bring him his slippers and robe when he gets cold
The Doctor just handed me a jewel, a precious little pearl
I'm as happy as I can be, because she's a girl

FALL

The trees are now bright with color
On the mountain stand they compete with each other
Their leaves are dry and ready to fall
They are waiting for the cold and the wind to call
Look, they are falling around
Yellow, orange, red and brown
They're beautiful; all colors are they
But the strong wind gusts will blow them away
Some leaves make tornado tunnels as they twirl
And the acorns have been stored away by the squirrels
I know I'll miss the greenery and the birds that sing
But they'll be back in early spring
All the leaves will be gone soon
In the dark we can see the autumn moon
At night the cloudless sky will be very clear
We know it's a sign; winter will soon be here

GRAY DAY

I'm in Seattle, this is a vacation; *But where did the sun go*
I could take a long drive into the mountains; *No I don't think so*
The weather man said tomorrow, partial sun and rain
To live here in this weather, you have to be insane
One year there was twenty-four hours of sunshine in twelve weeks
Depression and road rage were at their peak
I'm going to stick around for a few more days
And I would like to see blue skies but all I see are clouds of gray
It's damp and a little cold; *But where did the sun go*
I could take a walk on the Indian trail; *No, I don't think so*
I don't know if the sun will ever come out
But if it doesn't I'm not going to pout
I don't know if the rain will ever stop
And I still don't believe I've seen the last drop
I don't know how much more of this I can take
The people look fine but some things you can't fake
This weather has to effect the way they think
I'm pasted water logged and if I stay here I'll sink
It's dreary and the sky is getting darker; *But where did the sun go*
When I go back East, I could tell everyone to vacation here; *No, I don't think so*

TIME TO LEAVE

You should see yourself when you're on a drunken binge
You look more like what the dog took out than what the cat drug in
My mother told me not to marry you
My father said you wouldn't do
I know it was a mistake
Don't know why I did, for goodness sake
You acted like you were my jailer
But I made the payments on the pick-up and the trailer
I spent all day on my feet
I waited tables so the kids could eat
You went out with your friends for a beer
You didn't come back for a year
You think you come back like all is well
I don't want you back, you can go to hell
I'm making a new life for the kids and me
It's time to leave. You, I don't want to see
You are a dead beat drunk on a drinking binge
You look more like what the dog took out than what the cat drug in

LITTLE RED SCHOOL HOUSE

Down the dusty ruddy clay road there is a little red school house
The children sit at their desks, hands folded as quiet as a mouse
They look out the window at the covered water well
Over the double doors hangs a large brass bell
The teacher will ring it to call them to class
There are dark clouds overhead this good weather wouldn't last
Out back sits an outhouse it has wooden floors
There are large and small handles on each of the doors
Everyone is friendly, there are never any fights
On the front wall is a chalkboard where the teacher writes
She has a big desk, a pointer and keeps erasers in a trough
Children stay in at recess to clean the chalkboard if they goof-off
There is a potbellied stove in the middle of the room
The children sit at attention and they are all well groomed
No child would get into trouble, they wouldn't dare
They respect one another, the teacher is fair
First graders have short attention spans they are in the front row
The sixth graders sit in the back but they also have a need to know
Each student's desk has an inkwell and a swivel chair
I came here to learn, my mother and father care
I am in row one and my sister is sitting in back of me
She is four and I just turned three
The teacher is my mother's sister, schooling is a family affair
You can see some people have an advantage, life is unfair
We do our best, there are times we recite out loud
We must both do well in school and make our parents proud
You can learn about Shakespeare, about Caesar or Faust
You can learn all you need to know in this Little Red School House

BEYOND THE BLUE
A STORY FOR CHILDREN

There is a place that we all go beyond the blue
When life has been lived
There is a place that we all go beyond the blue
When life has been lived and we have not sinned
This is a magic place we will go
People who have not been good will not go beyond the blue
Beyond the blue a special place where everyone will be happy
All the parents must know that this is the place good children go
Just check in and give them your name
Because this is the place for fun and games
Grown ups can go too, beyond the blue
Some people grow and others grow up
Some people believe and why not
As long as there is a sliver of hope
We can all be forgiven and go beyond the blue

WINTER

This is the coldest season of all
It is better than the spring, summer or fall
My mittens, my scarf, my heavy coat and my boots
I wear over my swim trunks, my shorts and summer suit
I love the snow it is a beautiful sight
They say if there is snow on the grass in the morning it snowed in the night
I watch the snow flutter as it floats to the ground
The large white flakes stick together as they start coming down
I look out my window and I feel safe and warm
All comfortable and snug away from the storm
The snow has finally stopped and the night turns gray
I see a large evergreen silhouetted against the sky: it's the end of the day
I have settled down by my log fire in the cold of winter
With a glass of wine and a warm healthy dinner

A NEW YEAR

I should be happy, while I bring in the New Year
I'm sitting at a bar trying to drink down my fear
My girl said she was leaving me for some other guy
She walked out of my life and I don't know why
What did I do or say
That would make her treat me this way
I've had too many drinks and too many beers
I'd better leave now, hide my tears
I can't stop crying
Inside I'm dying
If she wants to go, then she should
It will be for the best, it will be for the good
I'm going for a long walk in the rain
I have to clear my mind, I have to clear my brain
I know it's party time, but I have to go
I can think about the New Year, in the rain where my tears won't show

CHARLIE BROWN

I'm a traveling salesman and I'm always out of town
When I come back early my girl has a frown
Billy-Joe, why don't my old bull dog bark when you come around
Why is the toilet seat always up and the blinds always down
We went to school, we were childhood friends
We made an oath to stick together through thick and thin
I don't trust you no more, I'm not rigid I can bend
But I feel like this friendship is coming to an end

You don't have to wear make up in a silly suite to feel like a clown
When I come back early my girl has a frown
Bill-Joe, why don't my old bull dog bark no more when you come around
Why is the toilet seat always up and the blinds always down
It doesn't take a college professor or a rocket scientist with charm
To know that he's been wronged and his girl has done him harm
I'm ready, I'm out of here, I'm going to lock and load

I'm splitting, I'm history, I'm going to hit the road
I got my pick up, my shot gun and my old bull dog to go
I'm gone, I'm tired of this dog and pony show
Early in the morning Bill-Joe, I'm leaving without making a sound
Because I know now why my girl had that frown
And I know why that old dog didn't bark when you came around
I know why that toilet seat was always up and the blinds were always down

A BAD HAIR DAY

I woke up this morning nothing is going my way
Rain is coming through the window and I'm having a bad hair day
I started to take a shower and the water went cold
My gray hair is standing up. The mirror makes me look old
I cut myself with that new mach II razor blade, it's so sharp
I wish my girl would use it on her legs because they feel like tree bark
I broke a collar button on my starched white shirt
It's my last clean one and I feel like a jerk
There is a spot on my best tie and a hole in my black shoe
The question, "To go to work or not to go to work?" I don't know what to do
Looks as if I'll be late I better get going
Well, it's only raining it could be snowing
I'm being positive I just got a new ride
I'm walking to the car it doesn't matter about the weather outside
My sock is wet from that hole in my shoe
I'll probably catch a cold or worst the flu
The driving rain makes my pants feel like a wet diaper
Hell, it looks like a parking ticket under my windshield wiper
The car seems to be, Oh no, I have a flat
I'm going back to bed on my bad hair day. What do you think of that?

SPRING

Snow, snow, snow, please go away
Let the sun come out and make a beautiful day
The water runs off the melted snow
There is a chill in the air but soon it will go
Summer is the warmest season of the year
But for now it's spring, summer will soon be here
The snow is gone but the ground is wet
A sign spring is around the corner, it's a sure bet
Yes, spring is close have no fear
The first signs of life will soon appear
Young sprouts are shooting up through the soil
They reach for the light as they uncoil
The buds are coming out on the trees
I'm waiting to see the first honey bees
I see a robin, spring is very near
Soon other birds and the bees will appear
When all the birds return from their winter retreat
I'll build them a house with a feeder so they can eat

ACTING ON THE STAGE OF LIFE

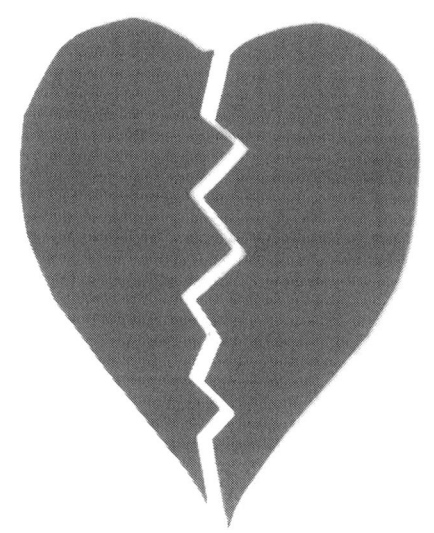

ACTING ON THE STAGE OF LIFE

I'm an actor in the theater of life, I'm on the stage and it's only a game
On this stage there is diversity, heartache and pain
Failure is not an option; at the end of that
tunnel is eternal darkness and shame
I want joy, I want happiness, and I also want fame
If I don't succeed, I know I only have myself to blame
Is there a path that leads to enlightenment?
Will I find peace in this land of enchantment?
Where will this all end?
The answer to that question is death my friend
Are fame and money the most important things in this world?
Or is it marriage and children with that special girl?
The answer to this question is they both are
Live in the moment, eat, drink, and be merry for tomorrow I die
I'm an actor in the theater of life, I'm on the stage and it's only a game
On this stage there is diversity, heartache and pain
Failure is not an option; at the end of that
tunnel is eternal darkness and shame
I want joy, I want happiness, and I also, want fame
If I don't succeed, I know I only have myself to blame

PARENTS KNOW BEST

Your father didn't like me because I was poor
He told me not to come back and knock on your door
Your parents knew what was best for you
A boy without family or money would never do
They picked your husband and set you up for life
But isn't living without love too high a price?
You were my Cinderella in a pumpkin carriage
Now, your father is giving you to another in marriage
At midnight you didn't turn into a chamber maid
You will always be my princess in a gilded cage
I've got to let it go, I can't stand the pain
I can't go there again I know I'll go insane
When you walk down the aisle with him, think of me
Look into your heart and it's my image you'll see
I hope you can be happy and fulfill all of your dreams
I know your parents have chosen for you, a man of means

LEAN ON ME

I love to ride in my red wagon, my brother and me
To share the joy of being with thee
Together we push and pull the wagon up the hill
Are we not all our brother's keeper?
We jump in, away we go, hoping not to spill
There could be torn pants, skinned elbows and knees
What joy, what fun, what glee
I love to ride in my red wagon, my brother and me
We hit a bump, we are out of control
Over and over, down we roll
I love to ride in my red wagon, my brother and me
What were we thinking to do such a thing
Is this a childish prank or a midlife crisis fling
Does the ride sum up most peoples life
My brother and me, we just got up and tried it again

ROUGH WEEKEND

It's early in the morning, I have a headache and I want to sleep
The alarm went off and I better get on my feet
Because the dog is restless and has to go outside
No, I'll get another wink, put my face under the pillow and hide
The canary and the fish should be fed
But I don't know if I can get out of bed
I'm going to be late if I don't get going
But it is cold outside and the wind is blowing
I think I hear something, it's just the snooze alarm
I'll lie here a few more moments, there's no harm
I bet it's very cold; what will I wear?
I've got to get up and take these curlers out of my hair
The blue dress is fine but the black one is better
It will go well with my turquoise sweater
I bought both dresses because I couldn't decide which one to keep
I'm calling in sick, it's a bad day and I'm going back to sleep
I really don't feel good; it's all for the best
I didn't want to go to work anyway; because I need my rest

IN MEMORY OF A SPECIAL PERSON
STEPS IN THE SAND

Life is short, we must live it fully, not in the shadow of death, not in fear
It is important to find something to live for because all life is dear
When you are gone, will you be remembered? Did you take unnecessary chances?
Do you want a small funeral or a large one with pompous circumstances?
Do you want people to think of you and cry?
Or celebrate your departure and look up at the sky?
Will you look back at the past, saying I wish I had; not realizing dreams
Did you frolic away precious time, when at your fingertips were the means
To waste your potential is the greatest tragedy of all
If you don't follow your star and answer your call
What has your life been about? What have you left behind?
Have you paid all your debts? Have you committed any crime?
Are you ready to go to the next world and start anew?
Or should the flames of the future be fanned with a notice of things still to do?
Think while you live what life is about for every woman and for every man
Or your last legacy will only be, fading footprints in the sand

ONE WAY GLASS

Do we set rules to keep things as they are
Do we catch a bus or are we chauffeured in a Bentley car
Do we set the rules to preserve our spoils
When there are changes do we get upset does our blood boil?
Is the one way glass in place because of prejudice and fear?
We don't want those people to get to close or to near
Different people, different things' are we afraid or we don't understand
Are the haves willing to kill, will they fight to the last man?
Do they feel anxious and want to keep their world as it is?
Do we all not like titles; Doctor, Mr., Mrs., or Miss?
I wonder about the one way glass
Does it depict value, importance or class
Do the haves care about the have nots?
Do they care if they sleep on the ground, the floor, a bed or a cot
It's a one way glass with the have nots on the other side
They have no place to go, no place to run to, no place to hide
Maybe the haves think only of the one way glass
Because they want things to stay the same for the future as they are in the present
                          And they were in the past
The haves don't really care if the have nots eat cake or if they eat grass
Because the haves will always change the rules to keep those people on the other side
                          Of the glass

ESCAPE

One must know what to salvage
If you follow your heart will it take you to a distant star?
Is there a price to pay or can we escape to afar?
What if we can not return?
Is the universe to large, to great, to vast?
Are there empty black holes and empty spaces untold?
What is out there; who knows, are there floating souls?
I am without hope in a land of plenty
Is there no hope for mankind?
Will I find salvation in time?
Is there a planet out there where I can find peace?
Here on this planet there is turmoil, disorder, destruction?
But in the end we have no shooting star to follow
We must all find peace, love and contentment on earth
There is no place to hide from one self.

THE ANIMAL LOVER

Some things are hard to understand
Even for a grown up man
Why would any one want to carry a rabbit's foot on a chain?
The rabbit with three legs was not lucky; the whole concept is insane
I'm thinking of a horse shoe over the door
Why? What's the reason? What for?
What happened to the horse? We know the rabbit is probably a dead duck
Did the horse throw a shoe; better the horse than me
It is all a play on words that I hope you see
Did the rabbit become a glove lining or maybe a rabbit stew?
Think on it, they turn old horses into glue
Ah terrible things, what's an animal lover to do?
Ridding on a cool fall day along a forest trail
The smell of the horse sweat is strong
The animal lover thinks putting a saddle on this beautiful animal is wrong
There is an established food chain and there are animals of burden
Maybe animal lovers should become vegetarians

A BITTER OLD MAN

I look in the mirror and what do I see
A bitter old man looking back at me
But how my face looks doesn't relate to my soul
I could be plain and young. I could be handsome and old
Is the man in the mirror good or is he bad
Is he happy or is he sad
Who is he and where is he going?
Is he a learned, all knowing?
Is beauty skin deep or is it deeper?
Who is my savior? Who is my keeper?
Am I a passionate person? What kind of scholar am I?
When I see the world's injustice, inside do I cry?
Why does God let these things happen? I wonder why?
I know the truth but it is not what I want to hear
It does little or nothing to alleviate my greatest fear
There may be no God, no one in control
In this world of injustice; we must help each other
                            Or stand alone

THE FALLING STAR

Look out at the universe, the vastness, the dark empty spaces
Look at your career, put your head down, come out of the blocks
You're off to the races
Always remember everything comes at a price, debts are paid
Forgiveness should weigh heavy in your heart when concessions are made
Think back, people said you were great, the
crowds, that look in every adoring face
You never thought it would end this way when you started this race
Now it is over
Glance back at the universe, it was once your world
Was it all a dream, did it really happen? Stand back, look, see the view from afar
The black holes, the streaking meters, an occasional falling star
In the end when you look back only you know how far you've come
And who you are

DOING THE RIGHT THING

What is on the other side of the moon?
Do we all have a dark side; what should we assume?
I get angry. Can I forgive? Am I tolerant?
Are some things unforgiveable?
Maybe some people can not be pardoned
Some feelings bring hope, some feelings bring fear
All things are not as they appear
You should hold it together, you must keep up your nerve
Some feelings should be held in reserve
Some feelings we don't admit to ourselves
Because they are buried beneath our mores of good
We know what we need to do; we know what we should
It's not as easy to do the right thing as it may seem
If you don't have the tools or at your fingertips the means
In doing the right thing there is a price we all pay
It may take from our families and cause us pain every day
We must reach deep down, it can be difficult and wrenching to our soul
And how much we suffer, how much we give up, only we will know

THE WORLD

Is it too difficult to live in the real world?
Do we seek alternative realities to escape?
Some people can see the future
Vampires must have human blood
Werewolves come out during a full moon
Aliens come from outer space to visit
Bogey man will get bad children
Ghosts return from their graves
Heroes shoot webs or wear capes and fly
Space ships travel beyond the sky
People visit other worlds where horses are in charge
Some people are immortal, never to die
Genies with flying carpets grant wishes on request
Our entertainment, violence, crime stories is this civilization's best?
Is there an Atlantis? Do people live beneath the sea?
Who has the lock on the truth, what is the future, who has the key?
The only thing that is certain, most commercial news is bad news

CROSSING THE RIVER

I'm crossing the river. What's on the other side?
I want someone to hold my hand I'm afraid to go, I'm going to hide
I'm walking beside the river and soon it will be time to cross
Now, I'm above everyone floating in space, I know I died
I'm a child of eight. I know there is much to know
My life is all ahead of me. They wait on the other bank soon I have to go
There are things I want to do, things I want to see, people I want to meet
Why do I have cancer, why do I have to die today
Why must it be me, why me, why me, what more can I say
Can't God change these things, find another way?

WHAT IS THE TRUTH?

What is the truth?
Does a stork bring babies? Is there a Santa Claus?
Untrue facts yell similar results
What we know as children is not what we know as adults
What is the truth?
If I know the truth what is there to fear
If I know the truth where do we go from here?
We must reexamine what was told to us and what the adults said
False stories, false facts should be put to bed
I am an adult now. I have to look at all the facts
I will make a decision and that is that
Things said in the past about matters is done
But my decision will be based on truths and things to come

WHERE IS HE

Taught me to accept what I couldn't change
Gave me a new understanding of mental pain
Thoughts are racing through my mind
I pause to think from time to time
I'm looking for God in the sky, behind every tree under each stone
In my heart, my soul, my mind I know he is gone
Taught me the meaning of hope and despair
In the end I really don't care
I'm in a dark place my mind is racing
Can't make it stop, stand up, now I'm pacing
Hope is important, life is short and for all those who believe
Death is a part of life so one must have time to grieve
Despair is when hope is gone
In the end I really don't care, God is lost to me and that is wrong

LOYALTY

When a loved one is in trouble and you can't change their circumstances
You have to put depression, anger, frustration and pain aside
All of these feeling you should hide
You must watch from a distance and swallow your pride
Or you will not be able to help that loved one,
if the times comes when you can

ALWAYS REMEMBER GREAT EXPECTATIONS
CAUSE GREAT DISAPPOINTMENTS

THE GOOD AND THE BAD

Where there is darkness, there is light
Where there is joy, there is sorrow
Where there is good, there is bad
Where there is a heaven, there is a hell
Maybe without hard times we would not appreciate the good times
If life was always bliss and a bed of roses
If there were no disappointments and no failures
If there were no set goals and challenges
If there were no heaven, or no hell
Maybe life would be dull and not interesting
Was the best you could do not enough and you failed?
Was the opportunity to try enough?
Was the failure accepted and is your heart contented?
Was the thought of heaven and hell on your mind?
Maybe without an effort there can be no meaningful success
Is there a heaven, is there a hell?
Is there the worst of bad times and the best of good times?
Is there a time in our life when you feel the good and the bad?
Is there a future heaven or a hell?
Or do hell and heaven exist only while we live!

A LEAP OF FAITH

Some people believe because they need to believe
Some people are followers and not leaders
They can make a leap of faith
Some people don't believe
They can't make a leap of faith
Thou shall not kill but Jesus was crucified and killed
He had faith
Those who follow his teachings must be protected by others
Do they have faith?
Some who have a religion kill others who have a different religion
They have faith
Do religions bring us together or do they separate people?
They all have faith
Their religion will past down from generation to generations
All have faith
Do prophets live forever?
They teach the faith
Is it important when the prophet was on earth or if he existed
Or is the message more important than the man when we
Make the leap of faith?

DOTAGE CRS

I came upstairs, now I forget why am I here
It's early in the morning and I'm trying to get my mind in gear
I'll stand and talk to myself, maybe it will come clear
Don't panic, I'll remember, it will come to me, there's nothing to fear
Can't recall but I came up here to get something I need
Hopefully, not like the Supreme Court's *In Immediate Due Speed*
What it is, I don't know, but it goes down stairs
I'll think about it, might as well sit down in this soft comfortable chair
Hell with it, I'm going back down
This really upsets me, I feel like a clown
But if it was all that important I would know what it is
I'm not going to stand up here all day giving myself a quiz
Maybe it will come to me if I stand up for a while
Damn, I'm old and frustrated, I feel like a child
Well, it's not coming to me and I'm in the middle of the room
I feel strange, it must be that time of the month, you know, probably a full moon
Well in your old age this is the price that we all pay
I'll go back down the stairs and stay
Maybe I'll come back up stairs later today
It couldn't have been all that important anyway

THE TREE OF WISDOM

I'm looking for the tree of wisdom
How will it help me?
Where can it be?
I will look far and near
I would like to find that tree
There is knowledge to be gained
And many places to see
I'm off but where do I go?
I'm going to a movie, a picture show
Or I'll watch my TV
There is plenty of information there for me
I have the need to learn things that are new
The same old things just won't do
I think wisdom is here, it is all around us
Scurrying around, looking here, looking there, why all the fuss?
I'll look for that wisdom tree some other day
Or maybe this feeling will go way

DISCERNMENT

I'm casting the net of the future, I'm casting it near and far
I'm catching all harmful words I'm putting them in a air-tight jar
You may feel betrayed and you may feel you were deceived
When words are shot from the bow of anger they can not be reprieved
It is for the best, it is for the good because once they are caught
We can stop the suffering they cause, words are arrows. They are the
                    Vehicles of our thoughts
Hateful words create distance, they are painful, they are ice cold
They go straight to the heart and pierce the feelings held in the soul
Chose your words carefully when addressing a love one
Remember what ever happened, happened, what is done is done
                    The scene can not be reacted
Because once spoken, sharp words can never be retracted
It is better to take a deep breath, the harsh words you should save
The hurt will be ever lasting and follow you into your grave

A LASTING PEACE

It is late winter, no sounds of birds flying overhead
No sounds of birds singing to wake up the morning sun
No sounds of cars passing by; the stars are not out and the sky is haunting
It's quiet, it is dark, there is stillness in the air

The wind is cold on my face
There is a lasting peace

My mind has been racing; what have I been thinking?
A day at the office, another day of unpleasant work
Can I leave the work at the office?
Can I rest my thoughts of this hectic day?
The wind is cold on my face
There is a lasting peace
I am waiting on the platform for the train to go home
I will read the evening paper until I arrive at my station
The car is there and my house is near
The wife and the children will be waiting

The wind is cold on my face
There will be no peace

TO SMOKE OR NOT TO SMOKE

Tobacco is dangerous and bad for your health
It is a cash crop that brings many to wealth

> To smoke or not to smoke
> To live or not to live
> To die or not to die

I choose to smoke in my house and not offend others
If we smoke in public who will we bother?
All who dislike tobacco will pass laws to counter
Ah those who smoke in public
So they do not cause disorder
Smokers will not smoke in restaurants or in local bars
They can smoke in their homes or in their cars

> To not smoke and live
> To not smoke and die
> To not smoke is best

Smoking is hazardous to your health, it says so on the label
The government protects all of us from each other
Sometimes I wonder why they bother
But does one have the right to smoke and die
Or does one have the right to die and smoke

DEATH OF A HUSBAN

I wake up every morning crying
I miss him, I can't get him out of my mind
He passed away, he is gone
I make it through the day telling myself I'm fine.
Some people never find a true love
If I can make a minute, an hour, a day
I loved him, I loved him
Maybe this loneliness, this emptiness will go away
I look back and see how lucky we were
I found him and he found me
Most people never know that kind of love
Soon we will be together in eternity
I can't stop this crying
In my heart the vacuum will never be filled
I miss him, I miss him
I hope I find some happiness while I live

A LIFE TO LIVE

As I look up into the sky, death is always near
As I look down at the ground, my wife is buried here
I see life through a red haze of pain
I live moment to moment trying not to complain
Death would be welcomed it would unite me with you
At times I'm confused and troubled I don't know what to do
I must continue to exist and go my separate way
I must still make choices day after day
In time I will be with my true love
Nora waits for me patiently on a cloud up above
Life for me now is like a dream
It is not always perfect or what it seems
My days are flying by like hourglass sand
As they slip through my fingers and fall from my hand
Please God tell me, when, where or why
We all want to go to heaven but no one wants to die

CHINA
THE LAND OF MYSTERY

I want to go to a land far away
I'm willing to travel night and day
I want to visit a place of culture and mystery
A land with over two thousand years of written history
A land of learning, silk cloth and spices sublime
A land where the people's eyes are different from mine
Million and millions have yellowed skin and straight black hair
They all look alike, Westerners shrug their shoulders and say in despair
The land of the Great Wall and exotic cuisine
Where rice wine and the noodle reign supreme
The land where they drink tea instead of milk
Where they wear robes of silk
Gun power was made for colorful fireworks to light up the sky
Not to conquer, to put an army in the field where people might die
Some live on boats and never put a foot on dry land
Fishing birds have collars so they can't swallow but they eat fish when they can
Their boats wouldn't go straight they would list and sputter
They thought about the problem and invented the rudder
They call their sailboats junks, are they trying to be witty
They have beautiful palaces, carved jade dragons, a walled in Forbidden City
Mounds larger than pyramids where emperors are entombed
Huge piles of earth cover them so they can not be exhumed
The emperor is going into the next world surrounded by his military forces
His terra cotta warriors are buried with their horses
Without question China believes their oriental culture is the ultimate best
Many of their secrets will always remain hidden from the West

A DRINK

The alcoholic moth is on an enlightened flight
As it circles and circles the candlelight
The glow illuminates the cold still night
But the flame burns hot, the flame burns bright
For the drunk moth it is an attractive sight
If he gets to close he' II burn his wings
But he thinks flying on empty is a dangerous thing
If he's sober he should keep flying and pass this one by
It's a long fall to the ground, it's a good reason why
He can refuel with alcohol at this station
But if he can't fly straight he'll get a citation
Early in the morning his lawyer is called to get him out of jail
He's told to bring his checkbook so the moth can make bail
Remember the drinking elevator goes down to the ground floor
Think on it and if you can, get out before
Because on the bottom there's no way out, no windows and no doors

B L P
BAD LUCK PAUL

I'm not a person who sings a sad song
But every thing I do is wrong
Some times I look back at my day
When nothing seems to have gone my way
When I wish I had stayed in bed
Because I know there's a dark cloud over my head
You know I'm looking around for someone to blame
But some people don't know when to come in out of the rain

I never finished the academy like I should
Now I guess I'll never know if I could
I didn't graduate with my class
I felt good when I got married but it didn't last
I tried to talk to the man upstairs when I put in my order
I wanted a son but he gave me two daughters
The ups and downs of life are part of the game
But some people don't know when to come out of the rain

I lost my money and my apartment buildings
Because of heavy drinking and wayward living
I saved my old car and I saved my old clothes
I couldn't save my marriage but that's how it goes
I'm in step now, I know how to come out of the cold
Now learning life's lessons before I get too old
I been married three times, I keep trying, but this one is done
In the back of my mind I wonder if I will find the right one
Now that you've heard my sad song
You must admit that some people do every thing wrong
I'm not complaining but it's a (GD) shame
Some people don't know when to come in out of the rain

TO LIVE OR DIE

All those who die don't deserve to die
All those who live don't deserve to live
Some who live deserve to die
Some who die deserve to live
For some living would be worse than dying
Dying is easy when there is nothing to live for
Living is difficult when you are surrounded by adversity
When there is much to live for dying is difficult
When all is lost living is difficult
We have no choice but to reside in this body at this time
We may not look alike but we all wish the best for our loved ones
The same hopes, the same fears and the same dreams
But here we stand, Now we must make the best of it
To waste the gift of life is unforgivable
Who should decide who should live and who should die?
We are part of things that were, things that are, and the things that will be

AN OCEAN OF TEARS

I looked up and the sky was blue
Now I look up, the air is all smoke
Things appear hopeless, what can I do?
I take a deep breath, I can't breath, I choke
                My eyes fill with tears, an ocean of tears
                   I am helpless, alone with my fears
                The teardrops flow from the windows of my soul
                  I am drowning without air but only I know
I look down at the land and it was green
Now I look down, there is erosion and waste dumps
The ground can no longer filter the water
Much of the land has been divided into sumps
                My eyes fill with tears, an ocean of tears
                  I am helpless, I am alone with my fears
                The tear drops flow from the windows of my soul
                  I am drowning without air but only I know
Once the ocean reflected the sky
Now it is gray and streams are a dark muddy red
We can clean up the water but we dump garbage in it. Why?
We pollute and kill, soon all the fish will die
                My eyes fill with tears, an ocean of tears
                  I am helpless, I am alone with my fears
                The tear drops flow from the windows of my soul
                  I am drowning without air but only I know

JUDGMENT

Growing up, going to school and breaking a golden rule
And the way your friends treat you will change
Life's interaction with acquaintance, friends and family
An act of bad judgment and all will change
A happy life of marriage with children
One indiscreet exposed moment and all will change
A life of Sunday church and righteous living
And one misstep and all will change
It takes a lifetime to build a reputation
And only seconds to loose it

REJECTION

How do I move past the rejection, the pain
Is there no part of me that doesn't ache with the shame?
Now, I'm num, I don't hurt, the anger is gone
I'm at peace with my self, I know where I belong
It is at the table of loneliness with my fear
I sit and I think, my reality is here
Will I live the rest of my time with no one to hold?
Does true love come once to the young and the old?
Can I get through this lost love and move on; will it pass?
Will the hole in my heart ever be filled or will it last and last?
I am disappointed, I am very sad
In life you learn to take the good with the bad
Things happen, you are saddened if you care
Life is sometimes complicated, it is not always fair

A CALL TO ARMS

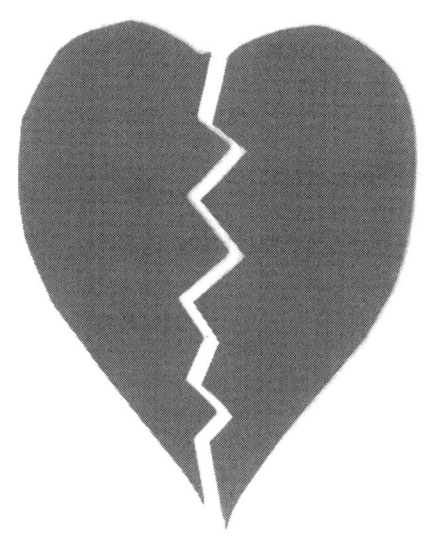

CALL TO ARMS

The band played and we all marched off to war
    We must fight so others may be free
    We must fight for God and our country
      The people shouted encouragement and our families cried

What is happening, why am I here, am I afraid, what do I fear?
Will I come back or will I die. Where am I going? I don't know why?
Will my girl wait for me. I must train in the Infantry
Will my girl marry or will she pine; I'll only be gone for a short time
Will my girl take a husband and have a child
If I'm away for a long while

    The band played and we all marched off to war
      We must fight so others maybe free
      We must fight for God and our country
        The people shouted encouragement and our families cried

Off we go across the sea by boat by plane to our destiny
We are now in different lands some have mountains some have sands
I have trained for many weeks and a good soldier I'll be
What will happen, where will I go, will I go down in history?
Who will take care of my dog; who will change the sheets on my bed
If I don't return it doesn't matter I will be dead

    The band played and we all marched off to war
      We must fight so others maybe free
      We must fight for God and our country
        The people shouted encouragement and our families cried

I am ready, I am here, to kill, to kill the enemy
Does he not have a family a sister a brother,
A father a mother?
Does he not go to church on Sunday and pray
Or is it on his carpet five times a day

    The band played and we all marched off to war
      We must fight so others maybe free

We must fight for God and our country
The people shouted encouragement and our families cried
The generals plot on the chess board to send men into battle
Soldiers are moved over the field of honor like herds of cattle
As the smoke clears, bodies lay broken, screams of pain, blood and tears
Helicopters, medics save lives but there are no cheers
Many men die, many are wounded and sent home
Those that survive bond together but in their hearts they're all alone
The band played and we all marched off to war
We must fight so others maybe free
We must fight for God and our country
The people shouted encouragement and our families cried
The war is over; I go home do I still have a wife
Will I have a job, will I have a life?
I would wave but I have no arms, a soldier I be
I would march but I have no legs and I can not see
We won the war but what was resolved, how many lives were lost?
The politicians pontificate and our loved ones say what a high cost
Where is the band that played when we march off to war?
Why did we fight to make others free?
Why did we fight for God and our country?
Where are the people who shouted encouragement when our families cried?

Is this life worth living or should I have died

ONCE I WAS A SOLDIER

The government declared a police action, they could
have declared peace, but they didn't
I wanted to be a civilian, but I couldn't
I wanted to stay with my family, but I couldn't
I wanted to stay in the United States, but I couldn't
I wanted to stay out of jail, I had to go or I couldn't
I wanted no killing, I wanted to run away, but I didn't
I trained with other men, I wanted to go home, but I couldn't
We became soldiers, my new family, I wanted to go home, but I couldn't
We were sent across the ocean, I wanted to go home, but I couldn't
We fought for each other, some were killed, I
wanted to go home, but I couldn't
I wish I had died with them, but I didn't
I wanted to cry, but I didn't
I wanted to be some other place, but I wasn't
I wanted to kill, I thought it would take away the pain, but it didn't
I wanted to bring back my new family, but I couldn't
I wanted things to go back to the way they were, but they didn't
I wanted to forget. I want to move on so the pain will go away, but I can't

LIFE/TIME

Life is movement through the weather
Good times and bad times
Good days and bad days
Rainy days and sunny days
The day begins with the rising of the sun
And it ends with the setting of the sun
There are sunny days, there are bad weather days
On the journey there will be friends, there will be others
A friend guilds you on the straight course through angry waters
There will be times when there is a lull in the storm
Everyday you live is a celebration of life
You must make a choice, are you dying everyday you are living
Or is it better to live everyday you are dying

THE DUFFEL BAG
THE ARMY WAY
(MOS) MILITARY OCCUPATION SPECIALTY

I look back and all I see is four years of agony

The gates of an army post are closing behind me

In my duffel bag is all I have and all I want to be

The light of freedom at the end of the tunnel gets dimmer

You're a GI now, Government Issue; you're assigned a number to remember

I hate moving from post to post

At times the move will be coast to coast

An MOS is who you are and what you do

A weapon will be assigned to you

In that duffel bag is all you have and all you own

Your orders tell you, what time and where to report to your new home

WAR

How much is a life worth? How much should it cost?
Another day with the smell of gun powder in the air
Another day of death and despair
Why am I here? Why do I care?
My country has sent me where few men dare
How much is life worth? How much should it cost?
I've crossed over the ocean to fight a brown man
In a land of desserts and drifting sand
Where stealing brings a penalty of a severed hand
Ninety percent of these people are illiterate and their religion is Islam
How much is life worth? How much should it cost?
Does one life hold more value than another?
Is an Arab son loved by his mother?
Why should men kill each other?
If we are God's children, are we not all brothers?
How much is life worth? How much should it cost?

WHY NOT?

I want to be whatever my ability allows me to be
If I have the ability I can be any thing I want to be
Why

I dream of being a football hero
If I was large, fast and strong
Why Not

I dream of being a lawyer
If I had an extensive vocabulary, intelligence and presence
Why Not

I dream of being a baseball player
If I had excellent hand and eye dexterity with speed
Why Not

I dream of being a doctor
If I had high intelligence scores and a will to save lives
Why Not

If we do not have the opportunity to follow our dreams
We can not succeed, maybe ability is not the only factor to be successful
Why Not

Different people have different skills
We are all equal but some of us are more equal then others
Why

THE ENEMY WITHIN

America the beautiful, the land of the brave and the free
My Country tis of Thee
The country that sent me across the sea
To fight for others' freedom that at home was denied to me
America was founded on principals of equality for all of us
Is it all a hot air balloon, a shameful bust?
Who are we and where do we go?
Why are we hated abroad, who runs this show?
Civilizations rise and fall
Great leaders make great calls
Decisions are made to reinforce egos, make men rich at an immoral price
Not to help the world's people achieve quality of life
In the past we had slavery, Jim Crow laws and segregation
American citizens, human beings were placed in degradation
The world was watching then and now, what more can I say
I hope we change direction and go a different way
There is a lot to own up to, debts we must pay
Americans must change for the future, we can
only hope God is not watching today

A CANDLE OF HOPE

As I live this life fighting through the tragedies,
the disappointments, the pain
The candlelight at the end of the tunnel is dim
The flesh of life clinging to my bones at times
only the thought of survival remains
As the darkness descends over my mind, my actions, my being
There is a candle in my heart that flickers
Life is on the table before me, on the plate of
all knowing, all hearing, all seeing
We must seize knowledge from life like starving
animals from a trough when they feed
The candlelight of hope burns brightest while charity and faith lag far behind
Charity and faith are pale reflections in the
mirror if there is no hope for mankind
All is not lost; we can find truth on the bottom
of the bowl of knowledge, if we drink,
if we feast, if we digest the fruits of wisdom
and realize hope is our basic need

IN THE SHADOWS OF DEATH

I'm a soldier and I am on a page of the book of life. Who wrote the story?
I walk the point. I walk the flank.
I was drafted and we are at war. I find excitement and I find glory.
But to take another man's life was not part of the Walt Disney story.
A soldier fights for his loved ones; he fights for freedom.
A soldier does his job; he fights for the man next
to him, they fight for each other.
On the front lines soldiers are brothers
He fights for honor, respect and for glory.
On the battlefield he blinks and another life is lost.
He is not there by choice. A year ago he was in high school.
Now he is in the game.
He has changed, his whole life has changed and he will never be the same.
Where did it all go?
Time may fly by but some things can not be undone.
If he had studied and gotten a deferment, he would not be there.
But he must focus, he does not want to get a
buddy killed, he lives one more day.
He thinks one mistake and all is lost because he is in a body bag.
He does not want to go home that way.

NO PAST, NO FUTURE, JUST NOW

I'm a soldier, this lady meets me in a hotel room
She is not my bride and I am not her groom
She makes love to me like there is no tomorrow
She has no conscience, no inhibition, no sorrow
When we are finished we go our separate way
I wait until she calls to set up another day
She is older and I know she's using me for her gratification
I'm tired of it, I want to get away, I going to take a vacation
I wonder what she sees in me
I should stop rationalizing, I know, but I'll go along and let it be
Lay back on the pillow, watch her leave and enjoy the ride
It's a beautiful day, pull up the shade and look outside
Realize with her there's no past, no future, just now; when I get her call
No picket fence around our house, no children, just the present, that's all

LIVING ON THE OUTER EDGE

Fear is an aphrodisiac
The rush of uncertainty causes great excitement
Some men live longer in a war minute than others in a life time of peace
On the outer edge is a life of brightness, eternal light
How long can a scintilla of light survive?
Is the spark of life so weak that the wind of fortune will easily extinguish
                                        Its light?
Some people die quietly, some people put up a long fight
Is the thread of life so fragile that it can be
broken with a single gust of wind?
Do we fly around the flame of destruction to increase the value of life
                              And the intensity within?
On the field of war if we burn our wings, we fall to certain death
Is the price of admission worth the final test?

WISH TO GO HOME

I'm a soldier called to arms
To trained and cross the sea to face bodily harm
Good-by to my wife, my son and my daughter
What fortune awaits over the water
All I leave behind, off to a land where people are frozen in time
Will I die in an Arab land? Will I die on a dune in the sand?
A land where men wear dresses and fire their weapons into the air
A land where they wrap rags around their heads to cover their hair
A land where the women cover their faces and are no more than chattel
A land where men treat women worse than we treat our cattle
Nine out often can't read, write or reason
These people live in a country of sand storms and winds with one season
In America we dress as we please, we can win money on a TV quiz
Their customs are different. I fight for their freedom
but I don't think they know what that is
These people hate me, the United States and what I stand for
The US, the Commander and Chief has sent me here to this War
But America is *MY COUNTRY* and I love it so dear
I hope I don't realize a soldiers' greatest fear
To die in this Godforsaken, foreign land and be buried here

AND LIFE GOES ON

Men inarch off to war, to lose life and limb *My Country Tis Of Thee*
They return home in pieces in body bags or with broken minds, from over the sea
Who will put them together again, what is next, what kind of life will they lead?
Were their efforts and sacrifices in vain; lives destroyed, the end of their seed
And life goes on. Who sends our young men to war; who said they must go?
Who makes this policy, who has the last word, the final say so?
Do the rich pay as high a price as the poor?
Or do the powerless and the minorities pay more?
Do the wealthy place their children where they don't have to fight?
Do they have the means for them to leave the country and take flight?
In the Civil War men could buy their way out of conscription
Today it appears nothing has happened to changed that depiction
As our youth perish in foreign lands do politicians attend affairs and boast
Or do they feel the pain like the families who lose the ones they cherish most?
Do politicians put obstacles in the road of life for self gain?
Do they have no conscience, do they have no shame?
No, they litter the path we walk with fallen trees, with sharp rocks and boulders
And life goes on; the flames of political vanity are fed with the bodies of soldiers

PTSD
(POST TRAMATIC STRESS DISORDER)

I'm home from the war in one piece. I made it back whole
I don't want to stand outside, looking in from the cold
I want to take my place in society
I want to blend in and leave my past behind. I want to be free
But I'm troubled, if I close my eyes war is all I can see
Somewhere out there is a safe place where I can be me
Broken bodies, burning flesh, men dying, the shame
Mass killings war fought in Gods' name
In my dreams, I see floating body pieces, dead
friends' faces, their agony, the pain
I can't forget, will I ever be able to sleep again?
At times it is more than I can bear
All the body bags going home, the dead enemy on the battlefield,
Someone should care
The carnage, the blood, the smell of gun powder in the air
The images, the noises, the ring in my ears
Thoughts spinning in my head, vertigo, the fears

Where in the world is there peace and quiet
I have to get away, get outside of my mind
A place with calm sea, wind not blowing, the people friendly and kind
No angry faces, no loud noises, that is the place that I'm trying to find
But I'm trapped in this nightmare with no way out, I'm screaming inside
But no one can hear
All I can see are burning bodies, the sound of my
pounding heart and I can smell the fear
Things are closing in on me, it's getting dark, there's a thunder storm outside,
I've got to get away

I can make it if I take it a day at a time, the migraine headaches, the pain, I deal
with every day
I know only hopelessness the heartache, the loneliness, despair,
Only I know
It has passed, I'm OK now, I'm going for a walk
in the rain where my tears won't show

A NEW WAR

My God is Christian forgiving, he is gentle and kind
Your God is Muslim, he is different from mine
Your God says to submit but he is cruel
My God is merciless too. Is that why they rule?
Our Gods tell stories that mislead
There is no excuse for those deeds
If we follow blindly in life and survive at all cost
We will pay a high price if our souls are lost
I want my God to be a God for all
For the world's children large or small
Can't our Gods now stop war, disease and pain
If they are *all knowing and all seeing* as they claim
We must have a holy war and bring disbelievers to their knees
Then we will have peace for our Gods, this I believe

THE PEACE POEM
A FIRE IN THE FOREST

Wars are started by the fears, the ambitions and the promises of old men
Wars are fought by the fearless, the ambitious and the promising young men
At home the old men pontificate and pose for public scrutiny
While the young men fan the flames with their blood and broken futures
Do old men wish to capture a past that is lost
Or the last chance for adventure not knowing the cost
Do young men seek fame and fortune for deeds to come
Or are they escaping from the boredom of home life and things undone
To impress the children, our fathers, our mothers and wives
The loss of innocence, of time, of limbs and lives
The price is too high, the cost is too dear
Forgive your fellow man, hope, faith and charity have no peer
Please, no more talk of war from principled old men
Please, no more talk of war from zealous young men
All nations, all women, all children beware
Of all the old men who start the fires in the
forest to light up their darkling sky
All children, all wives, all mothers who care
For the young spark of life burns bright
Until settling in the ashes of unfulfilled dreams to die

THE AMERICAN WAY

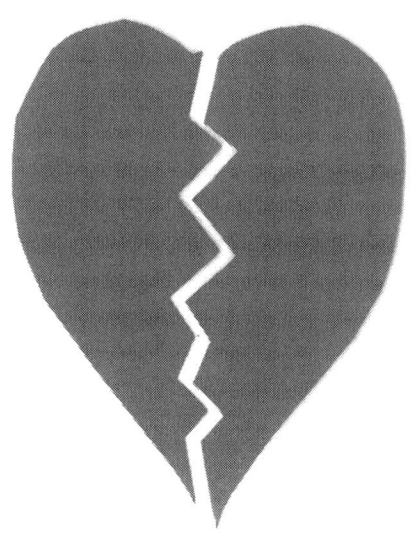

THE AMERICAN WAY

I'm looking at black history through tears of shame
Is the US a land of hypocrisy, empty promises, heart ache and pain?
Are all people treated with such disrespect? Who is to blame?
I look at the red man, extermination, lands taken, all lies
His treatment by the Europeans should be no surprise
The yellow man faired poorly as well
Building railroads, WWII internment camps, both a living hell
If God said all is forgiven, why treat people of color with kindness?
Doing the right thing for no personal profit is mindless
The fruit picked off the tree of charity is more desirable than the fruit
Of hate picked off the ground
Americans should always look up let others look down
An animal will live or die with the strength of its will to survive
But humans must have something to live for to keep hope alive
Our faith should sustain us. We should always
do the right thing, If we do our best
We will walk through the gates into heaven and that will be the final test
We all die some time it is only a matter of when
God will cleanse us all from our sin
We must forgive others and always remember
that battles and wars are fought but
The history is written by those who win

TRAIL OF TEARS

My family, my house, my land, my dreams are gone
For 12,000 years I lived here. Now I don't know where I belong
The White man's soldiers have taken everything from us but our souls
We gave him our women to marry, we spoke his language, we wore his clothes
        How far must we go today
        Will the soldiers let us stop and pray
        We walk West into the sun
My church, my house, my fields of grain are in flames
Our lawyer went to the Supreme Court, we won our case. Who is to blame?
Has our God turned from us. Does he think these people are best?
We have a written language, a paper and a printing press
        How far must we go today
        Will the soldiers let us stop and pray
        We walk West into the sun
Why is the White God so cruel; why has he turned his back to us?
I look forward, all my people and animals. I look back, clouds of dust
We fed the early settlers and taught them how to survive
They repaid us with treachery, guile and lies
        How far must we go today
        Will the soldiers let us stop and pray
        We walk West into the sun
We will all walk over 700 miles to Tahlequah
in heat, cold and snow on this trail
One in three will die on the way; the young, the weak, the old and the frail
These tears are for the White people who took our life away?
One day our God will turn to us and for the
White man it will be judgment day
        How far must we go today
        Will the soldiers let us stop and pray
        We walk West into the sun

THE BLACK PLEDGE

We must always remember who we were
We must constantly work in the present and always know who we are
Then we ensure a future where we will be what we can be
We are not what we should be
And we are not what we could be
But we are not what we used to be
We must participate in governing, voting and the administration of justice
An investment in this country of time, hard work with a vision of the future
Or we will remain visitors in the land of opportunity
Always remember who you were
Who you are
And who you could be
The past is important
To help us build and improve our life in the present
Because without a past there can be no future

INDIAN POEM

12,000 years here has earned us our name
We are Native Americans, we can hunt any game
We gave the whites corn and fish so they could survive
They repaid us with treachery, deceit and lies
They chased away our game, the bear, the deer
They killed our buffalo year after year
For Christmas they invited us to their fort to celebrate the day
They gave us trinkets and smallpox blankets then sent us away
They turned killer dogs on our women, children and the old
Their blood is warm but their hearts are cold
They drove us from our land, beaten and maimed
We lost our way of life, we were starved and shamed
Whites were single minded when they took our land
They forced us to live on the rocks and on the sand
They found gold in the rocks and moved us again
They have no feelings, no soul, no regret for their sin
Think on this, then tell me why
In all the Native languages there is no word for lie

DO WE REALLY HAVE A CHOICE

What does life offer to each one of us?
Do we really have choices?
If you could pick and choose, who or what would you be?
I am white, but am I?
I am privileged, I have advantages, but do I?
I can never be me
I am of color, but am I?
I am free, I am disadvantaged, but am I?
I can never be me
Why is America so racist and unfair?
Are we all clannish people who are naive and unaware?
The sickness affects our minds so we don't understand
We don't foresee 9-11's, we don't see an African or an Oriental as a man
Time is running out if we are to survive
Our children must come through this time period alive
With power comes responsibility and everything has a price
Americans' minds are not ready, the fortune wheels are still rolling the dice
We must realize civilizations are here for a short while
If they don't make the necessary adjustments they will not thrive
A species will pass, the Greeks, the Romans, we are not a crocodile

BESSIE SMITH

Where has God gone? Why has he forsaken me?
Where tell me as I die; where can my God be?
Where are the windows of my soul? Open my eyes so I can see
Because my skin was Black I was treated like I had leprosy
Much of my life as a blues singer was lived in pain and misery
I am dying and soon I will be moving to a better place
My blood leaves this body and I float into space
Death's door is open for me to come in
I have made my peace on earth; I am cleansed of sin
I have no regrets as I die today
I am ready for the next world; I have lived this life my way
My stay here has been wetted with rejection because I am Black
This should not be in America, but it remains a fact
I have but one wish as my soul leaves this place
We must live up to a civilized mandate, discrimination is a disgrace
Let all open their minds and eyes if they wish to see
Let the suffering, the despair, the hopelessness be
Let there be forever freedom for all the Black women like me

LOVE/DUTY, HONOR, COUNTRY

I want to leave this place
I know I can find peace some where
Should I give up on all people? Do I really care?
Or is it just this country that brings me despair?
I look and I see injustice every where
We must teach our children to stand up and be tall
They are created in God's image, large and small
But I see two factors that keep us apart
One is race, the other religion; you can see this if you are smart
Some people listen and some people hear
Some people are afraid of every thing different, they live in constant fear
We should build on our likeness and not dwell
on our differences in the human race
To look at any individual and prejudge them is an error, it is a disgrace
Each person is inherently unique and special in their way
A garden of many clustered colored flowers is something to behold
On a bright sunny day
There is a greater difference within racial groups than between racial groups
If you prejudge these differences, then you have been duped
We should give more weight to action than spoken words
All people should be treated as equals not as nerds
Americans should correct misdeeds against people of color,
We should address the wrongs
In time we will do this, our conscious is there and our will is strong
We as a nation can not undo what is done
But we can live our life and pledge to do better for
all people and a brighter future will come
If there is another (9-11) we will paint the future with their blood
We will fight for our freedom to the last man so
their Victories will taste as bitter as defeat
Every obstacle placed in our path we shall meet

If threatened we should bomb their country so only a blade of grass is
left standing and those who live will wish every minute they had died
We must look inward at ourselves with pride
It is better to die free men standing than to be a slave on your knee
It is the price we pay if we are to be free
I want to leave this place
I know I can find peace
Should I give up on all people? Do I really care?
Or is it just this country that brings me despair?
I look and I see injustice every where
After all is said, I think I'll stay here
I can't let things stay as they are, I can't let things be
I'll change what I can, God help us, my country tis of thee

EQUAL EMPLOYER

As we drive down the highway of life
We make decisions, it's a toll road, pay a price
Each of us is different, some are farsighted and some can't see well
Some are nearsighted and some are on the road of destruction headed for hell
Many see only the bumps a head, others can see the distant hills
We must stop now and then for repairs and gasoline fills
We can look to the left and we can look to the right
There are beautiful fields of grain, snowcapped mountains, breath taking sights
Others on this road; there are those who speed and pass us by
There are potholes in the road, there are valleys' low and mountains' high
Some stay in the fast lane while others drive too slow
Some drive a long way, some a short way and others stop and go
There are accidents, times we have to pull over and stop for personal reasons
There is rain, there is snow; we have cold, we have heat and the four seasons
On this road there is joy, sadness, good times and bad but there is no fairness
We are all unequally employed in the journey of life
As we drive down this highway there is only one guarantee for the trip
Death ends our employment because it's waiting at the end of the road

MIDDLE PASSAGE

I was stolen from my village and stripped to the bone
Destined to sail across the ocean in chains to lands unknown
I was sold to a slaver and marched to the sea
My wife, my sister, my daughter and me
They put us in a stockade until the ships came
We endured the heat, the stench and the pain
> *Where was God when they took me from my home*
> *Where was God when they took me to lands unknown*
> *Where was God when they took me across the sea*
> *Where was God when they sold me*

They stacked us in their ships with no space to spare
There was little water, little food, and no fresh air
We survived the middle passage, but were beaten with whips
And packed like salted fish in the hold of their ships
We were defiled, abused, killed and maimed
The passage took eight weeks, cruel and inhumane
> *I am not an animal who came out of a cave*
> *I have been violated and sold as a slave*
> *J was brought hobbled in chains to the home of the free and the brave*
> *I know God is watching; he will be care taker of my grave*

Sailors molested and raped the women in the dark
In the light they threw the sick and dead to the sharks
How can a man place such a high price on his life and so little on mine
How will my God in heaven punish this crime?
My country, my culture, my family, my name are forever gone
After 400 years here, I still have no place that I can call home
> *Some day I will find peace in afar away land*
> *Some day I will gather the bones on the ocean bottom sand*
> *Some day I will bury them beside their love ones so they are not alone*
> *Some day, yes, some day, some day, I will go home*

I'm trapped in my black skin with self-loathing and rage

With a mind set of a lion in a walled-in cage
Because of jim crow laws and prejudice my contributions to this country
                              Were ignored
If one man is denied his human rights, we all loose; the price an enlightened
                              Society can ill afford
I know only rejection and suffering until my life comes to an end
I look forward to death, death, it is my only friend

THE WIND AND THE WAY

Why has the white man come? It is gold he seeks
Why is the white God so strong? Why is the Creator so week?
The white man came like the stars in the sky
Over the big river, over the mountains like a forest fire
When the warriors were hunting for food for our village
They came with dogs to kill to burn and pillage
They invited us to their fort, feed us food, gave us dinner
Gave us small pox blankets to keep us warm for the winter
Eight of ten died because of their single mindedness and their greed
Who is their God, their Creator, what is their creed?
They kept one promise, they took our land, then killed all our game
They have no emotions, no conscience, no shame
Why has the Creator forsaken me
But in my dreams I am a nomad in my country, I am free
We were pushed west, freezing with no food, no hope, no land
The Ghost Dance at Wounded Knee was our last stand
The US made treaties, signed papers, they were empty promises, all lies
We were exterminated like rodents, insects, like flies
The US owes us money and will not pay to this day
And they don't understand why the world has no trust in what they say
If honesty and fairness are one's belief, they should be practiced at home
Or the world will turn it's back on the US hypocrisy and they will be alone

INDIAN THANKSGIVING

The pilgrims came across the great pond
They passed through the sun from far beyond
Their skins were white and they wore strange clothes
Did they appear from some distant land? No body knows
They came in big canoes that had giant butterfly wings
Their ships skimmed the surface like water bugs in the spring
These boats were long and wide and carried many braves
Flocks came ashore like summer birds over the waves
Some pilgrims had hair like straw and eyes like fishes
We wanted them all to go back where they came from those were our wishes
They gave us disease, they took our land and dreams, and had no shame
They lied, they cheated, killed our children, our women and our game
They told us one thing and then did another
There is no trust, they were not our friends or our brothers

IRISHMAN

I came to America in 1847 and here I am
Look at me I'm a human being, I'm a man
In Ireland my family was starving, we had no home, no land
The potato blight and the Whigs' Party left us no food
We had to eat raw shellfish, sea weed or face starvation
The voyage to America was our only salvation
Here there were signs, no Irish need apply
I look at my hungry children and I cry
These Americans are cruel, I don't know why
I came to America and here I am
Look at me I'm a human being, I'm a man
If I had a job I could feed my family
How can I give them clothing, food and shelter?
All I want is a chance to make a living
Where are the people who are loving, trusting and giving
This is the country of the land and opportunity
I came to America and here I am
Look at me again, I'm a human being, I'm a man

THE ILLUSION OF JUSTICE
RHYME AND REASON

Is the human race in the middle of a cyclone, a tornado, in a swirl?
Is there order in our microcosmic world?
Where are we going and how do we get there?
Should we look at all that is bad or all that is good and fair?
Are things predestined with no choices for us all?
Can we or do we make our own destiny, can we make that call?
Can we have order in the universe without justice?
We must have order first to create a Utopian society for all of us?
Justice has little to do with reality and love
We live in the sprit of the times; is each life set in place from heaven above?
Laws are the written rules to protect the powerful and the rich
A blindfolded lady balances the scales of justice; on the screen of life is she a glitch?
To survive we can create the allusion of justice as an aid
But we know justice is only equal to the amount of money paid
The poor are fantasize with justice and fairness because their life is so cruel
But for most, justice is a mirage on the horizon
of reality; that is a paramount rule

FREEDOM

It is not enough to open one's heart to love you
must open your mind and practice it
Everyday for a meaningful relationship

A single thought, an idea, a person never dies as long as
They live in the minds of the people

We are restricted at birth, by our genes
We are restricted as children by our parents
We are restricted when young by our teachers
We are restricted when adults by our education
We are restricted in life by our leaders

To grow the mind must remain open for new ideas
To listen, to process, to react, it is not enough to have the information;
You have to decipher and use to your advantage

Religion is the opium of the masses it allows them to view hope through
a narrow prism with tinted glasses, it can also be the most restrictive
institution for education and the most destructive instrument for war

We must learn to live together in peace on the planet as free people or perish
Apart as bitter slaves in the discontent of wars

All is done in moderation because too much living can cause early dying
The road to perfection is paved with many high expectations and shame
The road to Hell is paved with good intensions and pained

One should always be open to different religions. If we
can't live together we have only ourselves to blame

EPILOGUE

At the end of the day what have I accomplished?

At the end of the day what have I done?

At the end of the day are all things the same?

At the end of the day is anything different?

What can I do to make life better for all?

What can I do to make this a better place?

What can I do to help each person I meet?

What can I do to make me a better person?

There must be some good in all the people I meet.

There must be some good in a world full of pain.

There must be good in all of God's children.

We must find a way to help all of them.

Made in the USA
Middletown, DE
12 October 2022